the little do
up their
iles of th
coast in
ok at rag
oid
sir
pre
ailroad in
ue-
sky
h

SSAR

eru
ars
m

ng ex
he pa
p at
a
or Joa

m right
Henry a

white

the

n;

ly

seed, wi
grown on
seeds are g
and the re

AVE
350

Cin
LS

GIC

The Fact
ort Bui
co's P

OM
TOS

Cine

os legs

and is
s. The
moved
mixed

uction ry m
la Dijon
h

Presented to:

By:

Date:

My brethren, count it all joy when you fall into various trials,

knowing that the testing of your faith produces patience.

JAMES 1:2-3 (NKJV)

Columbine
ROCK-SOLID FAITH
Courage

Ron Luce

PHOTOGRAPHY BY GREG SCHNEIDER

J. COUNTRYMAN

NASHVILLE, TENNESSEE

Published by J. Countryman, a division of Thomas Nelson, Inc, Nashville, Tennessee 37214.

Compiled and edited by Terri Gibbs

Scripture quotations in this book are designated as follows and are used by permission:

New Century Version (NCV) ©1987, 1988, 1991 by Word Publishing, Nashville, Tennessee 37214.

The Living Bible (TLB) ©1971 by Tyndale House Publishers, Wheaton, IL.

The New King James Version (NKJV) ©1979, 1980, 1982, 1992, Thomas Nelson, Inc., Publisher.

The Revised Standard Version of the Bible (RSV) © 1946, 1952, 1971, 1973 by the Division of Christian Education of the National Council of the Churches of Christ in the USA.

Special thanks to Plough Publishing House, Route 381 North, Farmington, Pennsylvania 15437, for permission to use quotes from *She Said Yes*.

Designed by David Uttley Design, Sisters, Oregon.

ISBN: 0-8499-5607-2

Printed and bound in the USA

www.jcountryman.com

Teenagers have something
no other part of the church body does.
It's something like Timothy had—
they aren't willing to believe there's
something they can't do.
Tell a teen he can't dye his hair green
and he'll say, "Yeah, right."
If there's a Christian teen seeking the heart of God,
there's nothing that's going to stop him.

—TOM GILL

YOUTH MINISTER

Series Fraught
with ... tions

EDITORIALS

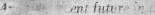

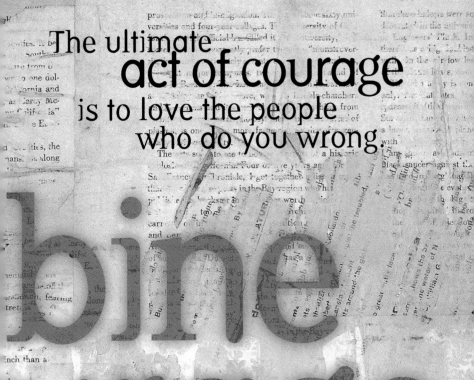

The ultimate **act of courage** is to love the people who do you wrong

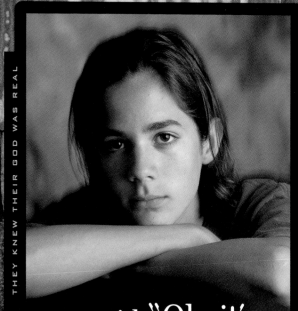

THEY KNEW THEIR GOD WAS REAL

They never said, "Oh, it's so hard to serve God. We have so much peer pressure."

No Matter What the Cost

Three young men, Shadrach, Meshach, and Abed-nego, were caught in the most incredible peer pressure you could ever imagine. These three young Jews were among the many captives who lived in Babylon. The Babylonians worshiped false gods and actually worshiped their king, Nebuchadnezzar, as a god. Shadrach, Meshach, and Abed-nego had peer pressure like you can't imagine. The entire nation was bowing down before an enormous statue, and these three who loved God refused to bow down, even though they knew it could cost them their lives.

In the midst of this incredible pressure they didn't feel sorry for themselves. They never said, "Oh, it's so hard to serve God. We have so much peer pressure." They stood with

9

courage, and they stood with valor because they knew their God was real. They had no hesitation in standing up for their God because they knew that every other god was false. The idol was a lie.

These young men chose to stand up for God no matter what happened to them. They set an example for you—for us all—to stand up for the truth no matter what the cost.

When my youth group heard about the shootings at Columbine High School we decided to pray for our school here in Los Alamos. We agreed to spend a couple of days praying, especially over the corner of the school where all the drunks and "druggies" hang out.

Well, we ended up praying for two weeks over that corner. We showed up before school every day and prayed over that area. The third week we decided we would also pray in that corner during our lunch break. During that prayer time, every single person in the group gave their life to God.

What used to be called the "Corner" is now called the "Christian Corner." All of that happened because of our prayers.

—ALICIA, STUDENT

NEW MEXICO

TURN THIS WORLD UPSIDE DOWN

God is raising up
a generation of young people
who are not satisfied with
the status quo.

The encouraging aspect of Columbine is that God is raising up a generation of young people who are not satisfied with the status quo in a culture that is quickly becoming morally and spiritually bankrupt. Drastic times call for drastic measures! In the midst of fear, this generation of young people is rising up to say, "Enough is enough"!! As hard as the enemy tries to destroy this generation, God continues to raise up a standard against him —this generation.

As tragic as the incident at Columbine was, young people all over this country are falling on their faces before God, pleading with Him to intervene. Along with this prayer goes a cry of "Here am I, send me!" May God turn this world upside down through this generation!

—JOSEPH, YOUTH MINISTER

Stand Up and Be Bold

J oel 2:28 (NCV) says, "I will pour out my Spirit on all kinds of people. Your sons and daughters will prophesy, your old men will dream dreams, and your young men will see visions." This is something worth turning our attention to; it's a great hope. The hope is that as we get closer to the end of time, God's Spirit will be poured out on young people and they will be used to make a huge difference in building God's Kingdom.

As a young person you need to embrace this promise and say "Yes, Lord! I am a part of that generation." After all, we are closer to the last days than we have ever been.

Now is your time to stand up and be bold because God is pouring out His Spirit to use you!

COLUMBINE

COURAGE

olumbine was a wake-up call for our youth group. We realize that being a Christian is not just something that takes place on Sunday, but is a real, everyday thing. Our young people are growing spiritually. Before Columbine they realized that people might have to die for their faith in China, but now they realize it can happen here in America too.

—JOY, YOUTH MINISTER
COLORADO

My friend and I started Fellowship of Christian Athletes two years ago. At the beginning of the 98-99 school year we started with fifteen people and were praying for more. We were doing pretty good with our little group on April 20, 1999. Things radically changed that day. While the shootings were going on at Columbine High School, I was listening to all of it over the radio. Several of the Christian leaders in our school and I got a group together and prayed for the students of Columbine while it was going on.

Well, the next week at FCA we had over thirty kids! The year finished stronger than ever with most kids having a renewed hope in God because of the dedication their peers, such as Rachel Scott and Cassie Bernall, had demonstrated at Columbine.

—JUSTIN, STUDENT
COLORADO

The day after the Columbine shooting, we took our youth group to a Christian concert. Three hundred teens went to the concert and seventy-two gave their lives to Christ. I have no doubt that the shooting had given them a new realization of life and death.

Kids are taking life more seriously now. Teens are more willing to hear about God and what He can do for them.

—DAVID, YOUTH MINISTER
WYOMING

WHAT CAN GOD DO THROUGH YOU?

God honored David's faith and gave him one of the most incredible victories in all of history.

An Incredible Victory

The story of David and Goliath (1 Samuel 17–22) is so awesome. It always amazes us that this little guy defeated a huge giant over nine feet tall.

One thing we sometimes forget is that David was a young man. The Bible says he was the youngest of his brothers (1 Samuel 17:14). That is why he was not in the war to begin with—he was watching his father's sheep. He was probably fifteen to sixteen years old. Naturally it would seem strange to King Saul that such a young person wanted to try to kill the giant.

But God honored David's faith and gave him one of the most incredible victories in all of history.

If God can do that through David, what can He do through you?

19

As a result of the Columbine High School incident, our student council made an extra effort to get students involved in school activities. We wanted to include everyone so no one would feel like an outcast. We encouraged cooperation between students so that everyone would get along. We also planned and produced more activities involving school spirit and pride. We wanted to create a sense of caring for each other in our school.

—MARK, STUDENT

TEXAS

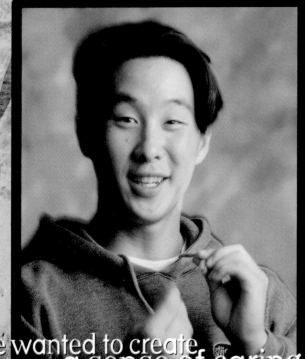

WE ENCOURAGED COOPERATION

We wanted to create
a sense of caring
for each other in our school.

"Until that day [at Columbine], I just took everything for granted. I pitch for the baseball team at school, and I took playing for granted. . . . I guess I looked at being a teenager as being immortal. As never being able to get hurt that bad, and definitely never dying, at least not for many more years. Now I can't think of it that way. I have to live today to its fullest, because I realize you can leave this earth at any given point in your life. It doesn't matter how old or young you are."

—JOSH

(THE SOPHOMORE WHO HEARD CASSIE BERNALL'S EXCHANGE WITH THE GUNMEN IN THE LIBRARY)

FROM SHE SAID YES

Make a Difference for God

A cts chapter 12 tells us how Peter miraculously escaped from prison and went to the house of some friends. He knocked on the door, but they couldn't hear him because of the noise of their prayer meeting. When they finally heard him and opened the door for him they were amazed at his escape and overjoyed!

One of the young people in the house that night was John Mark. He was right there to hear the incredible story of how an angel had opened the gates of the jail and let Peter out. Not long after that John Mark himself traveled with Paul and Barnabas on their missionary journey. He was probably about fourteen years old when he first traveled with them from village to village telling people about Christ.

He returned home and later went on another missions trip with Barnabas. Imagine him going to his mom and saying, "Please Mom, let me go on this missions trip. I know God can use me, and Barnabas wants to take me with him." Those early years of stepping out of his comfort zone marked John Mark's life forever. They were the start of a lifelong habit of making a difference for God in the world. Later in life, John Mark wrote a letter that is included in the all time best-selling book in the history of the world. You see, he wrote the Gospel of Mark.

John Mark made his life count for Christ even when he was young. Is your life counting for Christ?

What happened at Columbine was a turning point for One Way Youth. It opened up our youth to setting higher standards of living righteously. They have a desire to really seek God. They now have prayer meetings during the week and 90 percent of the youth group is faithful in coming. They love doing street ministry; going out and passing out tracks.

The enemy is trying to wipe out a generation. But this is *the* generation! God is raising up young people right now to take a stand for holiness and righteousness!

—ANNETTE, STAFF
ONE WAY YOUTH, COLORADO

HE CAN USE YOU

Would you consider stepping into the shoes of the disciples and going out?

God Always Goes with You

When Jesus sent seventy-two workers into His harvest field He said, "Go now, and remember that I am sending you out as lambs among wolves" (Luke 10:3, TLB). He was sending them out to preach throughout the villages. I think He was saying, "You guys are lambs. You're not even sheep yet. You're not old enough to be sheep; you are young, you are lambs." Maybe you don't feel very smart. Maybe you don't feel like you have it all together yet, but that's okay. God still wants to use you.

You see, because you are young, you are not hardened and set in your ways. You are still moldable, still pliable in God's hands and that is one of the reasons He can use you. Though you are young and feel that you don't know a lot of theology, don't let that keep you from stepping out for God. He can use you right now, right where you are.

———————————

Jesus sent the workers out to other villages to share the gospel. He wanted them to go out with courage. Would you consider stepping into the shoes of the disciples and going out to other villages or places around the world and taking the gospel on a trip this summer? Jesus didn't send His disciples out alone—and He doesn't send you out alone. He always goes with you. That should give you courage!

Columbine brought a revival to our youth group because it opened their eyes to the reality that living for Christ isn't just a church game. Not when you die for your faith. A lot of these students have become bold in their faith. They realize they don't have to leave Jesus at the front door of their schools and then pick Him up on their way out. He is always with them. They are beginning to see that their school is a huge mission field. It's not just up to their youth pastor to come preach. They need to be the ones to witness and share Christ with their friends.

—ERIC, YOUTH MINISTER
COLORADO

29

"**A**n event like this should cut us. It should change us. If it doesn't, there's something wrong. If you just let your life go on like it did before, you're burying a gift you've been given. You're missing an important moment."

—JORDAN, STUDENT, COLUMBINE HIGH

FROM SHE SAID YES

Rachel Joy Scott died at Columbine High School, on April 20, 1999, after declaring her belief in God. She was an average teenager except for her not-so-average walk with God. She had a passion for God and a passion for others.

To honor Rachel's commitment and courage, the churches of Sarasota and Manatoe Counties in Florida came together for a week of intense praise and worship and to be challenged to bring God back into our schools. It was called JOY week for Jesus-Others-You and for Rachel JOY Scott.

More than 700 young people attended nightly and some 500 decisions were made to live for God. The week was brought to a close by Heidi Johnson, a Columbine student who lived through the shooting. She challenged us to keep God's fire in our schools. Hundreds of young people wholeheartedly praised God and testified to their desire to know Him.

—JOE, YOUTH LEADER
FLORIDA

God had filled Rachel Joy with such love it permeated her life and those around her. Sometimes we think having a relationship with God is so difficult when it's actually quite simple. We just need to hold on to God and tap into His love. There is always more of God. Rachel Joy never stopped wanting more. That was shown to many thirsty souls through her life and death—something she could never have imagined God would do through her.

If our minds dwell on God, He will have a chance to work in our hearts in such a way that we can't help but have an intimate relationship with Him. God has so much love, joy, and peace for us it's scary. We cannot even imagine all He can do for us.

—ERIN, YOUTH MINISTER
FLORIDA

This is an excerpt from a letter that Rachel Scott wrote to a friend exactly one year before she died for her faith.

April 20, 1998

Dear _____,

It's like I have a heavy heart and this burden upon my back, but I don't know what it is. There is something in me that makes me want to cry . . . and I don't even know what it is. Things have definitely changed. Last week was so hard. Besides missing Breakthru, I lost all of my friends at school.

Now that I have begun to walk my talk, they make fun of me. I don't even know what I have done. I don't really have to say anything and they turn me away. . . . I know what they're thinking every time I make a decision to resist temptation and follow God. They talk behind my back and call me "the preacher's church-going girl." In the last 6 months my friends have changed. _____ thinks I am such a loser, and that God is just a phase for me. I have no more personal friends at school. But you know what . . . it's all worth it to me. I am not going to apologize for speaking the Name of Jesus, . . . and I am not going to hide the light that God has put into me.

If I have to sacrifice everything . . . I will. I will take it. If my friends have to become my enemies for me to be with my best friend, Jesus, then that's fine with me. You know, I always knew that part of being a Christian is having enemies . . . but I never thought that my "friends" were going to be those enemies. . . .

Always in Christ,

Rachel Joy

The more you allow God to make a difference each day in your life, the more your life will make a difference in other's lives.

MAKE A DIFFERENCE IN THE WORLD

God doesn't measure maturity by age but by obedience.

Never Too Young

Timothy was a remarkable young man whom God used in a huge way. We first read about him in Acts 1:1—5, when he heard Paul's preaching and God swept him off his feet. Timothy was probably only eighteen or nineteen years old, yet he just knew he had to make a difference in the world.

He began to follow Paul wherever he went and became one of his most loyal companions. Because he was faithful at such a young age and refused to get sucked into the rut of worldly living, he became more and more mature in his walk with God. In fact, he matured to the point that Paul trusted him with leadership over the church at Ephesus. Paul wrote two letters (1 and 2 Timothy) specifically to this young man to guide him in leading this church.

Paul held Timothy in such high regard that when he knew his own life was drawing to a close he asked Timothy to join him in Rome. According to Hebrews 13:23, Timothy himself was imprisoned for Christ but subsequently released.

What an amazing young man! His life is a moving example that God doesn't measure maturity by age but by obedience.

After the Columbine shooting our Fellowship of Christian Athletes really felt for the people who were hurt. So after school we had a prayer vigil. The awesome thing is that our principal came and was totally supportive. We prayed one minute for each teenager who was killed.

—MINA, STUDENT
COLORADO

REMEMBER THAT YOU ARE NOT ALONE.

He got active for God
and quit sitting around
feeling sorry for himself.

Standing Up for God

The prophet Elijah was really trying to follow God, yet he felt an incredible amount of persecution. Everywhere he looked people weren't serving God. Everywhere he turned people were persecuting him, mocking him, and making fun of him because he said he served a God who was so big and so awesome and so real. At first he felt bold and strong, but after a while the mockery began to take a toll on him. He began to doubt God and wondered if God was real. He became discouraged and cried out to God, "I have worked very hard for the Lord God of the heavens; but the people of Israel have broken their covenant with you . . . and only I am left; and now they are trying to kill me, too" (1 Kings 19:10, TLB). He was depressed and discouraged. He felt like he was the only person in the whole world who loved God and wanted to serve Him.

Do you know how God answered him? First, God told him to quit sitting around and get back to work. In fact, God sent him right out to anoint two kings and one prophet! God knew he would feel much more positive and upbeat if he got active for God and quit sitting around feeling sorry for himself. Then God gave him an encouraging reminder, "And incidentally, there are 7,000 men in Israel who have never bowed to Baal. . . ." (1 Kings 19:18 TLB). Isn't that great!

I'm sure this could be a true account for any one of you reading this book. Sometimes you feel like you are alone . . . like you're the only one who wants to stand up for God. But remember; you *aren't* the only one! In fact there are way more than seven thousand young people who are standing up for God. There are hundreds of thousands of them filling up arenas and stadiums. And then they are going back to their junior and senior high schools all over the land to serve Jesus Christ with courage, back bone, and fervor.

You don't know all of these young people but they are out there. Today on your way to school, remember that you are not alone. Be encouraged. There are thousands of teenagers just like you who love God and are standing up for Him today!

Because of the courage of the young Christians who died at Columbine, my daughter, Brittany, and three of her friends refused to read a book called "The Chocolate War" in their seventh grade class due to profanity, sex, and violence in the book.

—MISSI, MOTHER
OKLAHOMA

The tragedy at Columbine changed my ministry. It gave me a sense of urgency to bring teens back to God. I have sensed an outpouring of the Holy Spirit in our youth meetings like never before. Our teens want to be involved in ministry. They are beginning to share their faith by forming Bible clubs in their schools. And in our meetings at the church they are stepping up and taking more responsibility for the services. I am stepping back and merely guiding them. In fact we have formed a student ministry team that uses Genesis 50:20 as their base: "You meant to hurt me, but God turned your evil into good to save the lives of many people" (Genesis 50:20 NCV).

There is no greater time to be a Christian teenager. The change is exciting! The shootings were wrong, but the church is coming together to minister because of it.

—ROB, YOUTH PASTOR
COLORADO

Our youth pastor gave an amazing altar call right after the Columbine shooting happened. He talked about raising the standard just like Cassie did. It was a large youth rally that night and over 500 kids came to the altar. It was totally a move of God!

—JOY, STUDENT
OKLAHOMA

RAISING THE STANDARD

Over 500 kids came to the altar. It was totally a move of God!

The Columbine shootings had a great effect in the area where I live. The public school I attend had a memorial-type service outside by our flagpole the Tuesday we got back from vacation, and one of my teachers asked me to speak at this. I wrote a short essay giving a little background of Cassie Bernall, and a friend of mine read a poem Cassie had written the Sunday before she died. This was an amazing opportunity to witness to my entire school, students, the faculty and staff, as well as to news reporters, parents, and other townspeople.

The weekend before this event I had made a promise to God that I would be like Cassie. That I would stop "wussing out" when opportunities to witness came along. I prayed that God would give me opportunities to witness, but I had no idea it would be like this!

—ELIZABETH, STUDENT
MASSACHUSETTS

Obedient or Comfortable?

S ometimes your courage in standing up for the Lord will cause you to do things that might seem illogical to other people. After traveling all over the known world, preaching and enduring much persecution, Paul was headed back to Jerusalem. On the way back he stopped to say hello to some of the people he had won to the Lord. In many places the people warned him, "Don't go back to Jerusalem because you will be put in prison" (Acts 20 and 21).

But Paul answered them, "I am going to Jerusalem . . . not knowing what awaits me, except that the Holy Spirit has told me in city after city that jail and suffering lie ahead. But life is worth nothing unless I use it for doing the work assigned me by the Lord Jesus—the work of telling others the Good

News about God's mighty kindness and love" (Acts 20:22–24, TLB). It's as though Paul said, "You know it just doesn't matter what happens to me. I have got to obey God and do what I know is right. I believe that my faith, my life, and my future are in God's hands."

What inspiring conviction! No matter what it might cost, no matter how hard it might seem, it is more important to be obedient to God than to be "comfortable."

The day after the shootings we were at Clement Park just as the officials released the names of the students who had been killed at Columbine. Right then a group of about fifteen kids started praying and worshipping God. It was something no one expected. Another minister and I hugged these teens and joined in praying with them and for them. I looked around and saw about 150 to 200 students gathered and joined in worship. We were there for about an hour and a half. We gave an altar call and some students received Christ right there. It was awesome to see the students ministering to each other. The Spirit of God totally prevailed in that dark place.

—KERRON, STAFF
FELLOWSHIP OF CHRISTIAN ATHLETES

STAND STRONG IN THE FACE OF   PERSECUTION

Your courage will be shouting to them and the message can't help but be noticed.

The Message Will Be Noticed

I n Acts 2 we read how the Holy Spirit came upon Peter and many of the other disciples right after Jesus had left them. As a result, they began to preach like crazy, and God worked all kinds of miracles through them. No matter how many times they were told not to preach, they preached all the more. One of the things that spoke loudest to the people who heard them was their courage and boldness (Acts 4:13). When they saw such courage it caused them to take notice of the message. They had never seen people so confident, so con-victed, so determined.

Today as you go to school and stand up for your faith people might not understand what you believe or why you believe. They may even want to ignore the things you believe.

But when they look in your eyes and see your faith and courage it will cause them to sit up and take notice. They will realize that if you are willing to be embarrassed or harassed and stand strong in the face of persecution there must be something real to what you are saying.

Even if they don't "hear" the message you share with them, your courage will be shouting to them and the message can't help but be noticed.

There is a real desire among today's young people to express their religious beliefs and to rely on their faith during these troubled times.

—JAY SEKULOW
CHIEF COUNSEL FOR THE AMERICAN
CENTER FOR LAW AND JUSTICE

55

Ever since day one when I chose to stand up for my generation I have been attacked by the enemy. But a few weeks ago my friend asked me to pray for her at school, and I was really nervous because nothing has ever happened like that before. So I said, "Sure," and now we pray in our library at school. We are praying for a bigger group to grow to a classroom and to a whole cafeteria of teenagers praying for our country and world. I want to stand up for my generation, and God has inspired me to do that. I love Jesus with all my heart.

—AMANDA, STUDENT
CANADA

What happened at Columbine made a huge impact on my youth group. It really brought home the importance of being prepared to always stand up for your faith. What the devil means for harm, God can use for good. The devil thought he was getting rid of some Christian teenagers, but what he did caused hundreds of teenagers to stand up for their faith instead of being wishy-washy. The shootings made them realize they are in a warfare, and there is no way they can lose, because nothing can separate them from the love of God.

—DARLENE, YOUTH MINISTER

REACH OUT TO THEM IN LOVE

The ultimate act of courage is to love the people who do you wrong.

The Ultimate Act of Courage

J esus was the ultimate example of courage. Countless times in His ministry people mocked Him and made fun of Him. But He didn't care because He knew He was right. He knew He was God's Son and He had a mission on earth. That's not cockiness; that's confidence. The ultimate act of courage was when He was arrested, given a mock trial, and falsely accused—yet He refused to lash out at His opponents. Even when He was sentenced to death and had spikes driven into His hands and feet, He looked down from the cross at those who had crucified Him and said, "Father, forgive these people, for they don't know what they are doing" (Luke 23:34, TLB).

The ultimate act of courage is to love the people who do you wrong. You may have every reason to strike back at those who have mistreated you or mocked you. But that would be the easy thing to do. The hard thing—the courageous thing— is to reach out to them in love knowing that they have been blinded by Satan.

Godly courage demands that you love those who persecute you.

Those dying for their faith at Columbine High School forced others to look at their faith, the need to share Jesus' promise of eternal life with others, and the seriousness of the decision to follow Christ.

—ERIN
YOUTH MINISTRY

I had grown tired of the mediocrity that plagued not only my youth group but the entire sect of Christianity. Wasn't Christ all about giving His all in all? And yet we, the "little Christs" were sitting idly through service after service never following our leader with a fervor. Maybe I was just having one of those Jesus freak moments . . . but why not? Didn't He call each of us to leave our comfort zones, pick up our crosses, and follow?

A moment was all it took. I wanted a revolution to come ripping across my generation, but I knew it had to begin with me. "Lord," I prayed, "I want to start this revival. Please open a door for me and give me the boldness to walk through it." Slowly, I began to hear music filtering through my cluttered mind. I recognized it as a song that was very familiar to me: "Deeper." Tears began filling my eyes as the words echoed in my head. "I wanna go deeper," that was my prayer!

After the song I grabbed a microphone and started talking about changes that needed to happen in our youth group. The fire that God had given me could not be suppressed one more second. I put forth the challenge to go deeper with God, not just farther. That night, because of a simple act of obedience, about twenty people took up their crosses and threw off their worldly burdens. At that moment I realized that a revolution starts, not in one act of defiance but in a simple act of obedience.

—JENNY, STUDENT

OHIO

During my eighth grade in school I began to pray over my meals. People who were supposedly my friends began to make fun of me. Usually people are embarrassed when their friends make fun of them, but it wasn't like that for me. I turned to them and said, "Are you making fun of me because you don't know God and how to pray to Him?" One of my friends replied with an answer, "Yes." So I invited her to my house and taught her how to pray and brought her to God.

—MEGAN, STUDENT

OHIO

God Can Use Anyone

]magine the courage of Moses. He had been raised in Pharaoh's house his whole life and had the opportunity to inherit the kingdom. He could have had all the power and riches that a kingdom would offer. Yet after he discovered he was of Hebrew origin he had a decision to make. He walked up on a fight and saw an Egyptian beating up a Hebrew. He made the decision to jump in the middle of that fight and made sure it wouldn't ever happen again (Exodus 2:11–12).

Years later, after God spoke to him in the burning bush, he had to make another decision—God asked him to return to Egypt and face Pharaoh . . . to stand up for God's people. Now Moses was a human being just like you and I. He had doubts about himself just like we have about ourselves. "Lord," Moses pleaded, "I'm just not a good speaker. I never have been, and I'm not now . . ." (Exodus 4:10, TLB). But he finally said yes to God and with great courage and divine power stood before Pharaoh to bring God's message.

Anybody who has ever done anything great for God has had to make the courageous decision to stand strong against all the odds. Today is your opportunity to make the same decision to do what is right—to stand up for God even though you might face rulers and leaders at your school or job who don't love God at all. You see, God doesn't say you have to have tremendous talents or abilities before He can use you.

He will use anybody who will step up to the plate with courage and make the decision to stand strong for God . . . regardless.

I live twenty minutes away from where the Columbine shooting took place. A week after it happened I went to a youth rally with my church youth group. All of our hearts were changed when we saw how many of the Columbine students were there with soft and loving hearts for God. We made a banner for every student in the hospital and everyone signed it.

We made a dare to everyone in the youth group that we would step out of our clique of friends and make a new friend with a boy or girl in our school who always sits alone without a friend so that something like Columbine wouldn't happen again.

—ELIZABETH, STUDENT

COLORADO

This is part of an essay titled, "A Martyr is Born" that Aaron, who lives in Minnesota, wrote as an assignment for his English class:

Amidst the horrible shootings that have been plaguing the nation shines out a beacon of light. This light that provides hope and encouragement is God. In a society that is very godless, we must have the faith and courage like Cassie Bernall, who was killed in the Littleton massacre on April 20th because of her faith in God. She was one of forty-seven youth from her church who attended Columbine High School, and she was the only one who did not walk out alive.

Her brother found a poem in her room that night of her death that was written two days prior to the shooting. It reads:

"Now I have given up on everything else.
I have found it to be the only way
To really know Christ and to experience
The mighty power that brought

Him back to life again, and to find out what it means
To suffer and to die with Him.
So, whatever it takes,
I will be one who lives in the fresh newness of life
Of those who are alive from the dead."

Here is a girl who wrote a poem basically stating that she would give up everything to follow and really know Christ, who died and was resurrected for her and for us. Her family and friends hope and pray that Cassie's death is a testimony to others what real faith is. It is so unfortunate that shootings as terrible as these happen in our society, but we must always keep our faith and hope.

After the Columbine tragedy our prayer club at school went from about five people to twenty-five! The principal and staff of our school finally accepted our group and even gave us opportunities to do more. Next year we will probably be doing "Prayer at the Pole" every morning!

STAND UP WITH COURAGE

God is
looking for people
who can't be stopped.

Stare Down Hardships

There is an amazing list in 2 Corinthians 6:4–10. Look it up in your Bible. It's a list of the things Paul endured for the sake of the gospel as he traveled and told others about Jesus Christ:

beatings	imprisonments
angry mobs	exhaustion
sleepless nights	hunger

He continually stared down hardships with courage. Nothing could stop him or discourage him or shut him down. Through challenge upon challenge he kept standing with courage, standing with faith, standing with fire in his eyes and a conviction in his heart.

Too many Christians slow down after the least little bit of persecution. After one obstacle they whine.

But God is looking for people who can't be stopped. Whose faith is so real they keep pressing on no matter what. People who won't stay down, who refuse to give up. People who stand up with courage and face whatever the enemy throws at them with dignity and honor because they know that with God they can never lose.

When the shooting took place our group was overwhelmed with feelings of shock and fear. How could something like this happen so close to us?

I challenged our young people to stop and think about how they were living. I asked them, "What does it mean to say you are living for Christ?" When I heard that the 911 call came to the police at 11:21 A.M., God impressed me to give our kids a challenge. I asked them to take a moment every day at 11:21 to pray that God would come and minister in their lives and their schools.

Now it seems that more and more kids in the high schools are looking at our young people and evaluating their lives. They have opened up to what our kids have to say and they are more willing to listen.

—TWYLA, YOUTH WORKER
COLORADO

Any change to our culture that is going to be lasting is going to come through a revolution among the youth. That's why Satan is attacking this generation more than ever before in history. But these youth are becoming stronger than ever before. I'm trying to prepare these students to reach their school as a mission field. They have four years in high school to minister, but Jesus' ministry was only three and a half years, so they have an extra six months! I am encouraging them to get creative and get the word out!

—ERIK, YOUTH MINISTER
COLORADO

Although I attend a Christian school, prior to the Columbine shootings, my Christian faith was not very strong. I was not totally turned on to God, though my parents had pushed me to learn about God all through my life. But on the day of the shootings I found myself wondering, Would I have answered "yes"? For the first time in my life, I stepped out in my own faith. It was no longer my parents' decision, it was my decision, and I knew for a fact that I would say, "Yes, I believe in Jesus!"

When I got back to school, I found out that others at my school had made the same decision. In fact, one girl from the school got up and began to preach to the student body about how they needed to open their eyes to the reality of their faith.

The next week we handed out flyers promoting Spiritual Awareness Week at our school. I was totally surprised to see how many people showed up. That week, 104 students rededicated their lives to the Lord and 52 students were saved. Even the cool kids who thought they were too good for God were at the front of the chapel weeping and crying out to Him. They were humbled like never before. This started a revival that spread through all of the youth of our school.

—SARA, STUDENT
COLORADO

I am able, ultimately, to see the loss of my daughter not so much as a defeat, as a victory. The pain is no less. It will always remain deep and raw. Even so, I know that her death was not a waste, but a triumph of honesty and courage. To me, Cassie's life says that it is better to die for what you believe, than to live a lie.

—MISTY, (CASSIE'S MOTHER)
FROM SHE SAID YES

GOD WANTS TO USE ME

God wants to move in a big way. I'm going to jump out there and trust Him!

Perhaps God Wants to Use You

When I think of courage, I think of Jonathan, King Saul's son. This young Israelite stepped right out in front of the enemy troops at the risk of his own life. What incredible courage!

One day the Israelites found themselves in the middle of the mountains surrounded by their enemy, the Philistines. The Philistines were going to starve them and cut off all their water and let them die. But Jonathan, who was fighting with his father's soldiers, had the courage to believe that God would deliver His people from their enemy. He said to his armor bearer, "Let's go across to those heathen. . . . Perhaps the Lord will do a miracle for us. For it makes no difference to him how many enemy troops there are!" (1 Samuel 14:6, TLB).

In essence he was saying, "Perhaps God wants to move and do something huge here. But how can He do something great if we are all huddled in fear? In case God wants to move in a big way, I'm going to jump out there and trust Him!" And God honored his courage. The Philistines began to run in fear because they had a vision that all the Israelites were coming out of the rocks and chasing them. When they started running in fear the Israelite army grew courageous and realized that Jonathan had gone before them. They defeated the Philistine army that day all because of one young man who dared to say, "Perhaps God wants to use me."

Today as you go to school or to work you, too, can say, "Perhaps God wants to use me. Perhaps He wants to do something huge through me as I stand up for Him." Wherever you go today, go with that "perhaps God" spirit.

BOLDUCMBIZME

BOLDUCRAGE

The Columbine shootings and a local bomb scare impressed on the hearts of several teenagers from a multi-cultural Bible club in California to reach out to their school. This was not just an emotional decision. They put their words into action. They decided to put on an outreach event called Action House. They prayed every morning for two weeks before the event and advertised it on T-shirts, balloons, chip bags, and posters. There was a lot of persecution. Their posters were torn down, and they were only allowed to have the event after school but they pressed on. They realized that it didn't matter if someone persecuted them because today might be the last day to witness to other kids.

Over one hundred teenagers came to this event and thirty committed their lives to Christ. As a result of the event there are now up to seventy teenagers who attend the Bible club.

—BOBBY, YOUTH MINISTER
JERUSALEM PROJECT, CALIFORNIA

BE STRONG AND OF GOOD COURAGE

You need to choose
to be courageous.

Courage Is a Choice

When Moses died, Joshua was appointed by God to lead the people of Israel. It was a huge job! That's why God told Joshua three times to be "strong and courageous" (see Joshua 1:1–9, RSV). God knew what Joshua was about to face. He knew that all the armies in Canaan were going to be tough and Joshua would need to be a courageous leader. So God said, "Be strong and courageous!"

Notice that God didn't *ask* him to be courageous. He didn't say, "Joshua, would you please be encouraged? Come on Joshua . . . please? I know you can do it." No, God said "Have I not commanded you? Be strong and of good courage" (verse 9). In other words, courage is not a feeling or an emotion—courage is a choice. And today courage is a choice for

COOL MOVIE

83

COURAGE

you. You need to choose to be courageous before you face the battle of peer pressure or persecution.

Choosing to be courageous *before* the battle is the key to being courageous *in* the battle.

I've challenged the teens in our youth group with the "Columbine Torch Grab." I challenged them to pick up the torch that Rachel dropped. This had such a tremendous impact on our youth group that they changed the group's name to "Torch Grab."

The Columbine shooting had a huge effect on the youth in our church. This year's See You at the Pole had over 200 people in attendance. That's twice as many as last year! Our youth group has increased in size, and teens who weren't even active in the church a few months ago are now participating in ministry.

Teens today are hungering for the presence of God. They are praying for their own generation, and that's the key to revival!

—BRUCE, PASTOR
COLORADO

HE HAS THE POWER!

Stand strong today and let Him use you to change the world.

God Uses Unlikely People

God often uses the most unlikely person to do His work. That's what he did with Gideon in Judges 6. It was a desperate time for the Israelites, who had been captured by the Midianites. God came to Gideon and said, "Go and save Israel from the Midianites! I am with you!" (Judges 6:14, TLB). But Gideon had a whole list of reasons why God couldn't use him. "My family is the poorest in the whole tribe of Manasseh, and I am the least thought of in the entire family!" (verse 15). Gideon was saying, "You couldn't possibly use someone like me!" But the Angel of the Lord looked at Gideon and said, "But I . . . will be with you! And you shall quickly destroy the Midianite hordes!" (verse 16).

God was saying, "You've got courage, and I have the

power. Now stand up and let me use you to make a difference in your world."

God still needs people to do His work. So forget all those reasons why He can't use you. If you have the courage, He has the power! Stand strong today and let Him use you to change the world.

mmediately after the Columbine shooting a group of
Christians from our school called everyone to come to
another "See You at the Pole." We announced it to the school
and shortly after we did, our school received rumors of a
bomb threat. But that didn't stop us from meeting. We had
close to seventy-five people show up, and it was awesome!
There were people there who hadn't been at church or Bible
study ever. It was very encouraging to all of us.

—ASHLEIGH, STUDENT

TEXAS

Shortly after Columbine, a threat began circulating at our school that on Cinco de Mayo gunners were going to come and give the Mexican students some "real independence." Community fear escalated so much that everyone started to plan to stay home that day. Our youth group, other Christians, and Christian teachers stood up and had many opportunities to share our faith and confidence in God's protection and control, and His salvation.

Well, eventually only 400 of the 2,000 students showed up. But the great thing was that while nervous personnel and police worried, a bunch of us Christians met right out in the open in front of the school and prayed. The principal watched us and fearing for our safety asked us to go inside. . . . We had permission to go inside the school and pray! (Ha, ha policitians!) We prayed all week, every morning and lunch!

—CARA, STUDENT
NEW MEXICO

Determined to Make A Difference

hen Paul and Barnabas went to the town of Iconium, they preached with such power that many Jews and Gentiles believed in God. Yet some of their enemies stirred up distrust among the people and said all sorts of evil things about them. While the natural reaction might be to flee that situation, Paul and Barnabas did the exact opposite! Instead of fleeing these obstacles, they "stayed there a long time, preaching boldly, and the Lord proved their message was from him by giving them power to do great miracles" (Acts 14:3).

What a great example for you and me!

Today as you face obstacles at school or work, let it affect

you the same way it did Paul and Barnabas. When they faced opposition, they clenched their teeth and got all the more determined to stay there and make a difference. So be full of courage today and stay there and make a difference.

*E*very morning last year our school Christian Crossfire Club would pray together around the pole. Then we decided to pray every single morning around the pole. Our group grew from nine to sixty people that year.

At lunch time on Tuesdays we would go to the local church and have a Crossfire meeting. One day my friends and I decided to take the railroad tracks to the church. While we were walking along the tracks, some guys started yelling at us, "Hey Christians! Going to church again are you?" Then they picked up rocks (big rocks) and threw them at us as hard as they could. I believe the Lord Jesus directed each stone out of our way because not one rock hit us that day. This is an example of our faith under pressure.

—NICK, STUDENT
ONTARIO

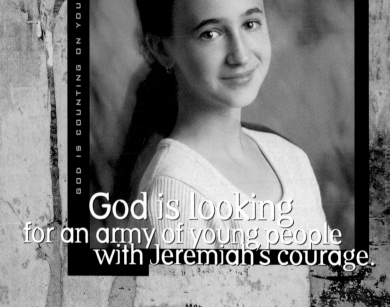

GOD IS COUNTING ON YOU!

God is looking
for an army of young people
with Jeremiah's courage.

God Is Counting on You

J eremiah, a timid young man, was called to be a prophet during a time of great storm and stress in the life of his nation, Judah. He was called to speak God's words to the people. God chose this young man for a challenging task, even before he was born. "I knew you before you were formed within your mother's womb; before you were born I sanctified you and appointed you as my spokesman to the world" (Jeremiah 1:4–5, TLB).

But Jeremiah thought God had made a mistake. He thought the job was way too big for him. "Oh, Lord God," he said, "I can't do that! I'm far too young! I'm only a youth!" (verse 6). But God rebuked him. "Don't say that," God replied, "for you will go wherever I send you and speak whatever I tell you to. And don't be afraid of the people, for I, the Lord, will be with you and see you through" (verses 7–8). In other words, God was counting on Jeremiah. He was counting on this timid young man to stand with courage and speak the words of God.

Today God is looking for an army of young people with Jeremiah's courage. Young people who will go wherever God sends them and speak whatever He tells them to say. Today as you march into school go with a "must" attitude. An attitude that says, "I must go wherever God sends me, and I must say whatever He tells me."

Don't say "I'm only a teenager; I can't be used by God." Don't say things like that about yourself because God is counting on you!

COLUMBINE

COURAGE

The incident at Columbine really made kids question their faith. It made them dig deep to find the answers themselves.

—CHRIS, YOUTH MINISTRY
COLORADO

After the shooting in Columbine, Jeremy, a middle-school student, and Chris, a high-school student, were impressed to take their school back for God so Columbine would not happen again.

Chris started a Bible study that had twenty students attending after just two months. Before Jeremy started a Bible study he went to the school leaders and sponsors to arrange for the group to meet at the school. The group was given permission to meet once a week for ten minutes. The principal went to Jeremy's mom and told her he was very proud of her son for taking all the right steps to start the Bible study. By taking all the necessary steps Jeremy won his principal's favor and support. The principal has already said he will help Jeremy set up new guidelines as the group increases in size. Both Jeremy and Chris are stepping out in boldness for God.

—JENNIFER, YOUTH MINISTER
OKLAHOMA

To the End of the End

E ndurance takes conviction, patience, and courage.
Jesus said that those who endure to the end will be
saved (Matthew 24:13). He knew that most people
wouldn't understand or accept the truth of His salvation. He
knew that those who did believe would suffer persecution,
would be betrayed, and even hated (Matthew 24:9). That's
why He said right up front that He is looking for people with a
fighting spirit and a heart that refuses to give up.

"Those who endure to the end." To the end of what? To
the end of the day? To the end of camp? To the end of their
junior year? No, to the end of the end. God is looking for those
who are in it for the long haul. Those who know that what they

believe is so real they refuse to be stopped. They will keep going until the end.

They will keep standing for God.

They will keep praying.

They will keep reading the Bible.

They will keep interceding.

They will keep fasting.

They will endure to the end no matter what persecution happens to them.

They walk through each day saying, "I'm not at the end yet so I've got to persist. I've got to endure no matter what hits me today."

God is looking for young people who are driven by conviction and courage. Teens who say, "I will endure to the end no matter what."

When Columbine High School had that massacre, it shocked me because it was in a high school in a little town. It truly opened up a door in my youth group. Our youth pastor shared some really awesome lessons and his vision to take us up to the next level of walking with God. Our whole youth group has been transformed.

In my own life, Columbine opened up my eyes. I have a new fire in my life. It's been in me ever since that day. I have been wholeheartedly telling people about God. I don't care anymore what happens to my body, because man can't do "jack" to me. I have a fire in my heart now that will live with me until the day I die.

—DAVID, STUDENT
ARIZONA

After the Columbine shooting the Christians at my school seemed to stick closer together. From the first day of school we had prayed together at our flagpole every Wednesday, but because of the hot weather and lack of interest, the group had dropped from about forty kids down to eight. Then, amazingly, in the weeks after the shooting there were more and more kids coming. Some had never come before. Isn't that awesome? So when it seemed that less people would take a stand for Christ, so many more did! Though we were scared, we gave our fear to the Lord, and He, in turn, gave us a new boldness to stand up for Him!

—NICOLE, STUDENT

TEXAS

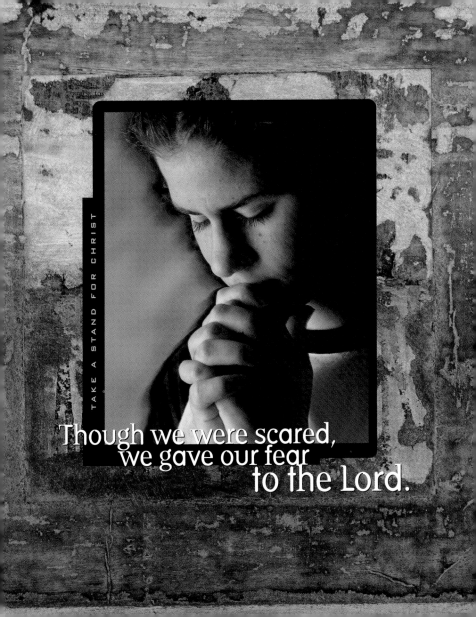

TAKE A STAND FOR CHRIST

Though we were scared,
we gave our fear
to the Lord.

Let Compassion Dictate Courage

When we face persecution our natural tendency is to flee the scene, to get away as quickly as possible and have nothing to do with that situation or those people. But when this happened to Paul, he went right back to the very people who had persecuted him!

It happened in a town called Iconium (see Acts 14:19–21). When Paul was preaching there, the religious leaders got the crowd all worked up and they dragged Paul out of the city and stoned him. They threw huge rocks at him until they thought he was dead and then they left him lying on the ground. Imagine Paul, lying in the dirt, bleeding and hurting after being pummeled with rocks again and again. But he didn't turn away from those people. The Bible tells us that he continued to preach the gospel in that area and a short while later returned to Iconium. Think about that. Paul went right back to the same people who had tried to kill him. What courage! What valor! What conviction! What compassion for those people, to go back and minister to them!

It reminds me of the story of David Wilkerson, a youth leader who ministered to the gangs in New York. One time a gang leader, Nicky Cruz, threatened his life, "We are going to cut you to pieces." David Wilkerson replied, "You can cut me into a thousand pieces and every piece of me will be screaming, JESUS LOVES YOU!" That melted Nicky Cruz' heart. Today Nicky loves God and preaches all over the world.

Let compassion for those who don't know Christ dictate your courage.

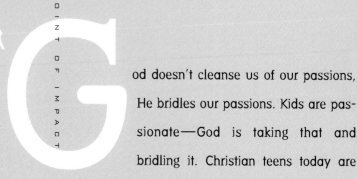

"God doesn't cleanse us of our passions, He bridles our passions. Kids are passionate—God is taking that and bridling it. Christian teens today are like a stampede of ponies under the control of the Holy Spirit."

—JOE WHITE
CO-HOST OF FOCUS ON THE FAMILY'S
LIFE ON THE EDGE

God Believes in You

t's impossible to stand with courage if you care more about what people think than what God thinks. In Matthew 13:3—8 Jesus told a story about a farmer sowing grain in his fields. The seeds represent God's Word, while the various types of soil represent the different ways people respond to God's Word. Jesus said, "The shallow, rocky soil represents the heart of a man who hears the message and receives it with real joy, but he doesn't have much depth in his life, and the seeds don't root very deeply, and after awhile when trouble comes, or persecution begins because of his beliefs, his enthusiasm fades, and he drops out" (Matthew 13:20—21, TLB).

This sounds like so many young people who go to a

camp or a conference or a revival where they hear enthusiastic words about following the Lord. They get excited and say they want to obey God no matter what. Then they go home and return to everyday life at school. As soon as someone makes a joke about their commitment to Christ or people criticize their faith, they lose their enthusiasm for following God. What seemed so real starts to die because they care more about what people think than what God thinks.

If we want to stand with courage we must listen to what God says to us rather than to what people say about us. We need to tune out all the negative voices and tune in the positive message of God's Word that says He believes in us. Then no matter what people say, it won't be nearly as important as what God says.

Courage isn't the absence of fear. Courage is believing that **God is bigger** than your fear. Courage doesn't mean you're **never afraid.** It means you take the things you're afraid of— whether people or situations— and you **face them head on** in God's power.

Here are some verses

to encourage you to stand strong for God.

The LORD is my strength and song, and He has become my salvation; He is my God and I will praise Him; My father's God, and I will exalt Him.

EXODUS 15:2 (NKJV)

Continue earnestly in prayer, being vigilant in it "with thanksgiving."

COLOSSIANS 4:2 (NKJV)

Rejoicing in hope, patient in tribulation, continuing steadfastly in prayer.

ROMANS 12:12 (NKJV)

Be anxious for nothing, but in everything by prayer and supplication, with thanksgiving, let your requests be made known to God; and "The peace of God, which surpasses all understanding, will guard your hearts and minds through Christ Jesus."

PHILIPPIANS 4:6-7 (NKJV)

My brethren, count it all joy when you fall into various trials, knowing that the testing of your faith produces patience.

JAMES 1:2-3 (NKJV)

COLUMBINE

111

COURAGE

Use the space below to write some of your

favorite Bible verses:

_____

_____

_____

_____

_____

_____

_____

_____

_____

_____

_____

_____

_____

_____

_____

_____

If you are willing to stand strong for your

faith in God, use the space below to write

a personal pledge of commitment to Him:

I pledge to _____

_____

_____

_____

_____

_____

_____

_____

_____

_____

_____

_____

one nt teen-
car varnin
am and
its
putti

zoo, M

had C

Ins an
talking

Fre

Ha
we

Bur

Handwoven
flat weav
linen warp
folk des
brown, Bu

on his
grea arnin

nology

rnia region, in

student

Through decor
ightweight

The eighth and

d heart A
Ca
und
n supper